Inventing with LittleBits

By Adrienne Matteson

Published in the United States of America by
Cherry Lake Publishing
Ann Arbor, Michigan
www.cherrylakepublishing.com

Series Editor: Kristin Fontichiaro
Reading Adviser: Marla Conn, MD, Ed., Literacy Specialist,
Read-Ability, Inc.
Photo Credits: All photos by Adrienne Matteson

Library of Congress Cataloging-in-Publication Data had been filed and is available
at catalog.loc.gov

Cherry Lake Publishing would like to acknowledge the work of the Partnership for
21st Century Learning. Please visit *www.p21.org* for more information.

Printed in the United States of America
Corporate Graphics

A Note to Adults: Please review the instructions for the activities in this book before allowing children to do them. Be sure to help them with any activities you do not think they can safely complete on their own.

A Note to Kids: Be sure to ask an adult for help with these activities when you need it. Always put your safety first!

Table of Contents

Each LittleBit piece does a different job. Put them together to make an invention.

How to Be an Inventor

Welcome to being an inventor! Inventors create machines that solve problems. Inventing is exciting and challenging. Inventors usually have to try over and over to get their machines to work. Do you have an idea? With the right materials, your invention could change the world!

Making inventions that light up is just one of the many things you can do with LittleBits.

How Can LittleBits Help?

LittleBits is a great tool for inventing things that need to be powered by electricity. It is a set of blocks called bits. Bits snap together with magnets. You can use them to build an electrical **circuit**. Do you want your invention to light up, make sounds, or move on its own? If so, you might want to use LittleBits.

When an invention makes something happen, like turning on a light or making a sound, that is an output.

Meet the Bits!

There are four kinds of bits:

- Blue bits connect your invention to a power source, such as a battery or a computer.
- Pink **input** bits send a signal to your circuit with a button or a **sensor**.
- Green **output** bits light up, make sound, and move.
- Orange wire bits make your circuit bigger or longer.

All it takes is two bits to create your first invention.

Making a Circuit

The smallest LittleBits circuit you can make is a blue power bit snapped to a green bit. When the blue bit is connected to power, it turns on the green bit and makes the light go on. It will also turn on the green bit. This is just like putting a battery into a new toy.

Lots of LittleBits

There are more than 60 LittleBits bits! Try out the ones you have. Do any of them remind you of tools and **devices** you use in your everyday life?

In this invention, a pink switch bit controls the light on the green bit.

From Circuit to Invention

Adding a pink input bit to your circuit lets you decide when the green bit is turned on or off. Think about how you want your invention to turn on. When you push a button? Flip a switch? Clap your hands? Different pink bits can change the way you control the green bit.

Testing Your Tools

An inventor checks every tool. Try out all of the pink and green bits to see how they work. Take notes as you work. You might need them later!

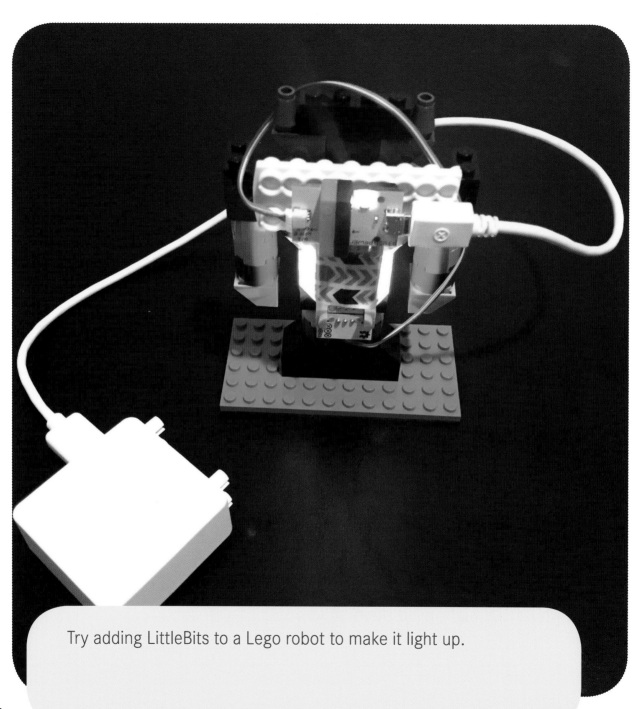

Try adding LittleBits to a Lego robot to make it light up.

More Materials

LittleBits work best when you combine them with other materials. You can use paper, craft sticks, cardboard, or almost anything else in your LittleBits inventions. You can even use brick **adapter** pieces to attach LittleBits to a Lego creation!

What other materials will you need to build your invention?

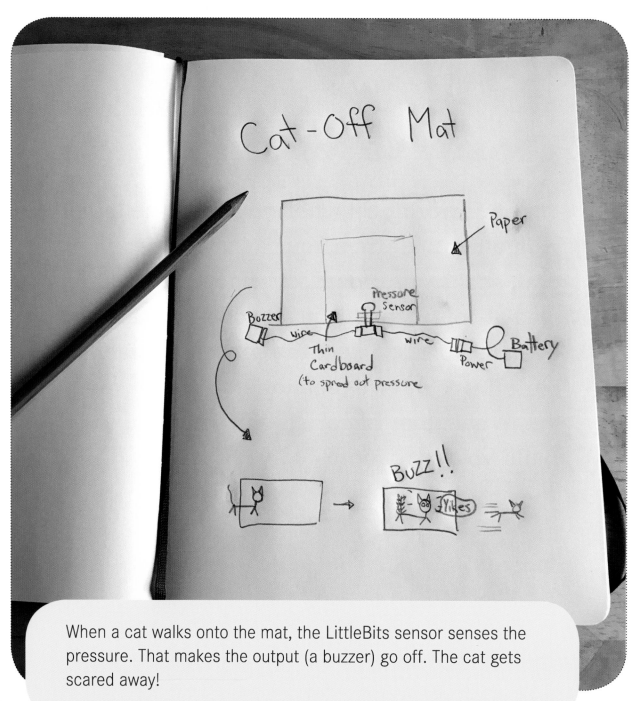

When a cat walks onto the mat, the LittleBits sensor senses the pressure. That makes the output (a buzzer) go off. The cat gets scared away!

Make a Plan

A good inventor does not usually just dive into a project. Instead, start by making a careful plan. Draw a **diagram** of your invention on a poster or whiteboard. List the bits and other materials you think you will need.

Everyday Inventions

Need an idea for an invention? Make a list of some problems you see every day. Pick one that you might be able to solve. Then give it a try!

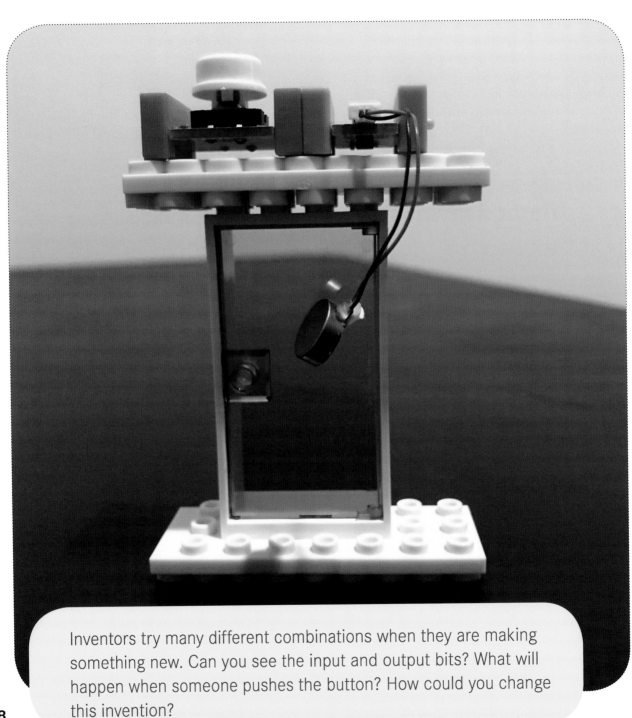

Inventors try many different combinations when they are making something new. Can you see the input and output bits? What will happen when someone pushes the button? How could you change this invention?

Try It Again and Again

An invention is never really finished. It can always be a little better. Inventing is a circle:

You will probably need to test your invention many times before it works like you want it to. Don't give up! Remember that mistakes can lead to great inventions.

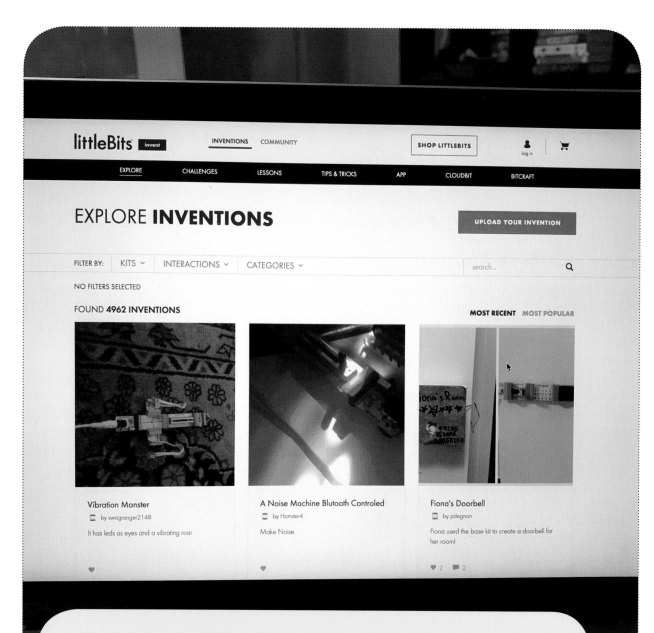

Check out the LittleBits website (*http://littlebits.cc*) for all kinds of project ideas.

Share Your Inventions!

The world needs your invention! Share it with your family and friends. They will be amazed. And they might have more ideas to help you.

The LittleBits website also has a place for sharing projects. Ask your parents if you can share your project online. You might help other inventors with their big ideas!

Taking Notes

Each time you test your invention, take notes and pictures. You never know when you might need your old ideas!

Glossary

adapter (uh-DAP-tur) device that helps connect two things that were not made to be connected

circuit (SUR-kit) an uninterrupted path along which electricity can flow

devices (di-VISE-iz) tools or machines that do particular jobs

diagram (DYE-uh-gram) a drawing that shows and explains the parts of something

input (IN-put) information that is put into a machine

output (OWT-put) light, sound, or other information produced by a machine

remix (ree-MIX) change something to make a new version of it

sensor (SEN-sur) a device that responds to light, touch, sound, and heat

Find Out More

Books

Lovett, Amber. *LittleBits*. Ann Arbor, MI: Cherry Lake Publishing, 2016.

Thomas, AnnMarie, Kristin Fontichiaro, and Sage Thomas. *Building Squishy Circuits*. Ann Arbor, MI: Cherry Lake Publishing, 2018.

Web Sites

LittleBits

http://littlebits.cc/projects

Explore the projects that other LittleBits users have shared online. This is a great place to find ideas!

LittleBits: Tips & Tricks

http://littlebits.cc/tips-tricks

Need some help? This web page is full of videos, pictures, and explanations to help you get to know your LittleBits better.

Index

About the Author

Adrienne Matteson lives in Atlanta, Georgia, where she teaches and sometimes invents things in her middle school library.